C

SanJuanita Escalera

BookLeaf
Publishing

India | USA | UK

Presentation by *BookLeaf Publishing*

Web: www.bookleafpub.com

E-mail: info@bookleafpub.com

ISBN: 9789358369434

First edition 2023

DEDICATION

To my loving husband Cristian, whose
unwavering support in my creative pursuits
have been a constant source of inspiration. To
my twin Elizabeth who has been with me and
writing since the beginning, and to my sister
and brother from another mother, Tiffany and
Eric, who were the first to lend their ears and
hearts to my poetic endeavors, I dedicate this
book to you.

ACKNOWLEDGEMENT

To my beloved family and closest friends,

Your unwavering support and love have been the driving force behind my writing journey. Your belief in me, encouragement, and presence have shaped this collection in immeasurable ways. I am forever grateful.

Forever yours,

SanJuanita

PREFACE

Through the simple and wonderful medium that
is language and the resonance of emotions, I
hope to make a connection that resonates with
your own experiences in your own journey
through life. I encourage you to embrace the
beauty and the complexity of your own feelings
and to find comfort and understanding in the
shared human condition.

Cup of Tea

I'm not everyone's cup of tea,
They have their elegant Earl Greys, soothing
herbals, and lovely green teas.
But what's my order, you ask of me?
Well, that's easy, you see, I don't like tea,
So just a coffee for me.

To be me

I am a masterpiece of my own design,
Uniquely crafted, one of a kind.
Embracing my flaws as life's reflection,
A tapestry woven with self-perfection.

I won't conform or bend my way,
For I am the master architect of my own day.
Living authentically, true and free,
In the joy of being so unapologetically me.

To be friends

Oh wow! No way!
Me too! You don't say?!
Here I thought I was the only one!
Join me, my friend, let's have some fun!

Best Friend

More than just a friend but not born siblings.
Though after you meet us, you'll know we are
closer than siblings. Always together, birds of a
feather. We're there for each other no matter the
weather. The closest of confidents, some even
say lovers, until our very last breath, is our
connection with each other. How blessed are we
to share this life until the end, you are after all,
my very best friend.

Let's Dance

Stolen glances at every chance, creating a
captivating trance.
Caught in the fiery embrace of destiny's hold,
A tapestry of possibilities waiting to unfold.

A million thoughts swirl in my restless mind,
Yearning for courage, a leap of faith to find.
With a racing heart and fluttering core,
It's time to act, to tread uncharted floor.

Summoning courage, I take a step ahead,
Leaving behind the realm of doubt and dread.
Oh, hesitant heart, seize this fleeting chance,
For fate has whispered its magical dance.

And in that moment, as if the universe heard,
A voice breaks the silence, my heart stirred.
"Excuse me," they say, their words a sweet
surprise,
"May I have this dance?" I meet their gaze,
mesmerized.

With synchronized movements, we become as
one,
The music guiding us, an intimate union spun.

Every step and turn, a language unspoken,
Our souls intertwining, barriers broken.

Underneath the moon's tender, watchful gaze,
We surrender to the rhythm, lost in a daze.
In this dance of destiny, our spirits ignite,
A tale of connection written in every graceful
flight.

So let us waltz together, fearless and free,
Exploring the depths of this newfound reverie.
For in the embrace of this enchanted romance,
We discover the magic of seizing life's dance.

Familiar Strangers

Friends for ever we would say. Always together
every night and day.
You and me against the world. Pinky swear, we
gave our word. Oh, if only we had known.
Now you're just someone that I used to know.

A pleasure to make your acquaintance

In a world of hidden glances and secret smiles, a thrilling game takes shape.
Like spies in a mission, we engage in this playful dance fueled by intrigue and excitement.
With a twinkle in our eyes and a mischievous grin, we exchange coded messages.
Each gesture carries a hidden meaning, a tantalizing invitation to delve deeper into this exhilarating connection.
Every stolen glance reveals a hidden layer of our desires.
We become agents of our own emotions, playing with fire.
Yet reveling in the enchanting danger of it all.
In this game of hearts, we find solace and excitement, knowing that the stakes are high, but the rewards are worth it.
It's a reminder that even in the midst of our daily lives, we can find moments of exhilaration and connection that make us truly feel alive.

Mornings

Five more minutes please, I don't want to get up!
This whole waking up early is all kinds of messed up!
My brain is not here right now, my spine left last night!
How is it time already I just said good night?!
"You'll be late!" Says the clock as I look at the time
So I rub my eyes and let out a ghostly sigh
I reluctantly agree to leave dreamland behind.
But in my sleepy haze, there is a glimmer of hope
A chance to seize the day to cope.
As I face the world outside, I let my tiredness slide.
Though mornings may test me, I'll find my way.
Embracing any challenge that may come my way.
But its Saturday! Say the calendar as I head for the door,
Oh, never mind then, I think I'll sleep a bit more!

Daily Grind

Just set the alarm,
How is it time to get up?!
Hurry you'll be late,
No room to mess up
Make this, handle that
Turn this in on time!
Bottling all this stress for what feels like a dime.
Battling the daily grind to put food on the table.
Most of the time it feels like I give more than
what I'm able.
No time to fall behind I have to do what I can.
Amidst the chaos, a tranquil space, my true
purpose remains.
 to provide and strive despite what feels like
growing strains.
For with each step forward I am build something
new,
Creating a life where all my dreams come true.

T.G.I.F

Thank the Gods its Friday, the day we adore,
Where work feels light, and worries soar.
Smiles widen, spirits lift high,
As Friday's arrival draws nigh.

Plans are made, excitement grows,
With friends in a row, the weekend flows.
Laughter echoes, music plays,
Friday nights, in vibrant arrays.

Release the stress, let loose and unwind,
Friday's magic, a treasure we find.
Dancing, singing, fun in the air,
Friday's here, let's live without a care!

Gone Digital

Unfollowed and unfriended, our connection is
gone,
Status change "in love" "single" "moving on."
Emojis that once sparked joy now bring tears,
In this digital realm, we face our fears.

Messages left unseen, conversations erased,
A virtual breakup, hearts left displaced.
our love, our timeline, funny memes, now a
memory,
Scrolling past moments, a painful reverie.

Unfriended, no requests and blocked profiles,
Digital wounds that will take a while.
But through this screen, we'll find our way,
To heal, grow, and find a brighter day.

Though pixels fade, our hearts still beat,
Learning to love offline, our true ultimate feat.
In this social media age, we'll rise above,
Embracing new chapters, like finding self-love.

Enough

In a world that demands perfection, this is truth I
say,
You are more than enough, in every single way.
Don't measure your worth by standards they'll
impose,
For within you, a radiant godly light already
glows.

You have no need of validation from others to
feel complete,
 Your essence is what makes you truly elite.
Embrace your flaws, your quirks, your beautiful
scars,
They tell your story, of how far you've come.

You are enough, just as you are, with all your
dreams and all your fears,
With every stumble, every triumph throughout
your years.
Your worth cannot be measured by
achievements or fame,
It resides within you, an eternal flame.

Your voice always matters, your presence has an
impact,

Don't dim your light, let it shine, and attract.
Embrace your strengths, your passions, your
grace,
For you hold the power to create your own
space.

Remember, beautiful soul, that self-love is key,
To recognize your worth, to set yourself free.
In this journey of life, with its twists and its
rough,
Know that you are, and always will be, enough.

Beloved

In your eyes, my world takes flight,
Cupid's embrace, shining so bright.
Your touch, a fire that sets me free,
With you, mon amour, I'm where I should be.

You are my anchor, my guiding star,
In your arms, I find solace, no matter how far.
With every beat, our hearts align,
Forever together, your hand always in mine.

I do

Two souls entwined, in perfect harmony,
Marriage's symphony, a sweet melody.
Hand in hand, we navigate life's maze,
Basking in happiness, through our joyous days.

Together we build a love that is strong,
A partnership enduring, never wrong.
In wedded embrace, we find our bliss,
A forever promise, sealed with a kiss.

Parting Ways

In the vast realm of love, where promises once
thrived,
Paths diverged; two souls contrived.
A story ended, whispers in the freezing breeze,
A tale of separation, searching for ease.
Two lives untangled, shattered hearts.
A symphony disrupted, notes gone awry,
A walk of separation, a somber goodbye.

Yet from the dark depths of pain, resilience shall
rise,
Like a beautiful phoenix, soaring in the skies.
For with each ending, new beginnings ignite,
A chance for growth, a radiant light.

Moving On

In the echos of what once was,
Lies a whispered tale of letting go,
Sometimes life blows wind on our sails,
Guiding us to move on for us to grow.

Like a bird soaring through the sky,
Leave behind what no longer serves us,
goodbye.
With wings unfurled, freedom calls,
A journey awaits, keep standing tall.

Embrace change, find our way,
Releasing ties that held us at bay.
The passing of time is a healing balm,
Moving on with grace, like a calming psalm.

Through tears and smiles, a heart is reborn,
Seeking the light of each new morn.
For in the tapestry of life's grand scheme,
Moving on is where dreams redeem.

So let go of what's been left behind,
Embrace the future, unconfined.
With open arms and spirits free,
We find our strength, and truly be.

A new kind of love

These past 9 months have been a rollercoaster
"You're glowing, everyone says, but no one
helps me with how to deal with my fears.
My body is not recognizable to me anymore; all
the changes shake me to my core.
"The most important job in your life," keeps
ringing in my ears as I struggle and wipe away
tears.
Months pass and I can't help but wonder if I'm
fit for this role,
Am I good enough? Will I still be able to be me?
I feel like no one is hearing me.
Suddenly everything is a whirl, the moment I've
been dreading and preparing myself for
Excitement and fear take over, begging the
heavens for the pain to be over
Suddenly the long time came to a stop
A cry in the air made my beating heart drop
I look in relief at the new life before me
For that moment my doubts and fears take flight,
like a dove
And for the first time in my life I'm engulfed
with a new kind of love.

Shimmers

Waiting for the sun to fall,
To witness the moon's shimmering glow.
Pondering if you truly had to go,
Memories rise in my head, standing tall.
On this Day of the Dead we tread,
I find myself wishing it were me instead.
The wind calls as the sun takes its bow,
Trees dance along, hearing its whispering vow.
And like a soft whisper, your presence appears,
Through my tears, I see the shimmering glow
clear.

Shadows

Not all days bring warmth and ease,
Some are cold, dreary, and bring unease.
But fret not and let regret subside,
These shadows will fade, for they cannot reside.
We keep going, keeping them at bay,
The sun will return, illuminating the way.

Goodnight

Alas, the day is done, the sun has set,
Stars emerge, embracing night's vignette.
Release the day's stress, let it slip away,
In the past it shall stay, as we welcome dreams'
sway.
Rest now, find solace in peaceful sleep,
Tomorrow's blessings and challenges to reap.
Remember, do what you can, let worries be
light,
For now, sleep tight, dream with angels, and bid
goodnight.

Only Human

In this wild world, we humans roam,
Messing up, learning, and finding our homes.
With hearts that feel, and minds that spin,
We're a species that's prone to all kinds of sins.

We stumble, we fall, gracefully yet so absurd,
Tripping over shoelaces, saying the wrong
words.
From awkward moments to funny mistakes,
We're a bunch of oddballs, whatever it takes.

With laughter as our medicine, our souls
unwind,
Tickled by life's quirks, the absurd we always
find.
We dance with joy, and sometimes cower with
fear,
Navigating this comedy show, year after year.

In this grand cosmic theater, we play our part,
Winging it through life, a comedic art.
From clumsy mishaps to comical strife,
Being human is a never-ending punchline for
life.

Printed in the USA
CPSIA information can be obtained
at www.ICGtesting.com
LVHW022313090324
773914LV00014B/968

9 789358 369434